THE
BANKING
BOOK

DATE DUE

the BANKING *book*

ELAINE SCOTT

drawings by

KATHIE ABRAMS

FREDERICK WARNE

New York   London

The author wishes to thank Charles A. Angel, Jr.,
of the Preston State Bank in Dallas, Texas, and George J. Watts, III,
of the Bexar County National Bank in San Antonio, Texas,
for sharing their knowledge of banking with her.

The illustrator would like to thank the Federal Reserve Bank
of New York, The New York Clearing House Association, and the
Chase Manhattan Bank NA for their generous help.

Frederick Warne & Co., Inc.
New York, New York
Library of Congress Cataloging in Publication Data
Scott, Elaine.
The banking book.
Summary: An overview of banking, its history, its
services, how banks earn money with your money, and
how banking laws ensure protection for your savings.
1. Banks and banking—Juvenile literature.
2. Money—Juvenile literature. [1. Banks and
banking. 2. Money] I. Abrams, Kathie. II. Title.
HG1609.S36   332.1   81-2412
ISBN 0-7232-6202-0   AACR2
Printed in the U.S.A. by Rae Publishing Co., Inc.
Typography by Kathleen Westray
1 2 3 4 5 85 84 83 82 81

For my father
GEORGE J. WATTS JR.
who understood that there
is much more to banking than
putting coins in a clay pig.

CONTENTS

THE
BANKING
BOOK

Medium of exchange for services

1

MONEY AND BANKING— HOW IT ALL BEGAN

*D*O YOU LIKE MONEY? I
bet you do. Money is important because it is a *medium of exchange*.
That means that people use money to acquire the things they want.
When you go to the store and exchange 20¢ for a package of gum, your
money is being used as a medium of exchange for goods—in this case,
some gum. Perhaps your neighbor hires you to feed her cat while she is
away for the weekend. She agrees to pay you $2.00. Again, the money
becomes a medium of exchange—not for goods that you can hold in
your hand, like gum, but for services. You exchange your services of
feeding the cat for her money. Bankers say that money is a medium
of exchange for goods and services.

Money is also used to show how much something is worth. A price
tag of $75.00 dangles on a new bicycle while roller skates are priced at

$15.00. The merchant is using money to show that the bike is worth more than the skates.

Another way money is used is as a *reserve*. Perhaps you have some money in a savings account in a bank, or in a piggy bank in your room. Maybe you add a few dollars to your account once in a while. You are not using your money as a medium of exchange, because you are not buying anything. You are not using your money to show what something is worth, because you're not selling anything, either. Instead, you are using your money as something bankers call a *liquid asset*. A liquid asset is something that can be spent right away, and money is the only completely liquid asset that people have.

People have other valuable assets, of course. You might own a nice stereo system, but you cannot take that asset down to the store and exchange it for the new bike you want. Your stereo system would have to be converted into cash first. In other words, you would have to sell your stereo system before you could buy the bike. Although your stereo system is an asset, it is not a liquid asset.

On the other hand, the money in your savings account is a liquid asset or *reserve*. A reserve is money on hand for immediate purchases. You can take $75.00 from your savings account and buy that bike right away.

Now that we're talking about money, I bet if I asked you to close your eyes and think about some, you would conjure up stacks of dollars, quarters, nickels, dimes, and pennies. I bet you would *not* conjure up stacks of feathers and stones. And yet, long ago, the people living on the

island of Yap in the South Pacific used stones for money, and the people in New Hebrides used feathers when they wanted to buy something. Those are some of the heaviest and lightest monies that have ever been used.

In the nineteenth century, the people of Borneo used palm nuts and pigs as a medium of exchange. Palm nuts and pigs were money to them. The most valuable money, however, was—ugh!—a human skull. After a while, the human skull became the *standard* for their currency, and palm nuts and pigs were used for the medium of exchange.

When something becomes a standard, then the medium of exchange—whatever it is—is measured against it. For example, in Borneo

perhaps ten pigs were worth one skull, while twenty-five palm nuts were worth one skull. Using the skull as a standard, the people could easily see that a pig was worth more than a palm nut. Historically, in the United States and in most of the western world, gold was used as the standard. (Aren't you glad we didn't use skulls?) And instead of pigs and palm nuts, we use coins and paper money as the medium of exchange.

Money has been around for a very long time. So have banks. Records dating back as far as 2000 B.C. show that the temples of ancient Babylon loaned people money, which is something banks do today. By 500 A.D., in Greece and Rome, institutions much like today's banks were accepting deposits of money, changing coins (and testing them to see if they were real or counterfeit), arranging for credit between cities—in short, performing many of the services that banks do today.

Today, as in the past, people use banks to handle their money. Your bank at home may be a pig with a slit in its back, but your parents' bank is probably a large building with plenty of armed guards and burglar alarms and heavy steel vaults, which protect the money and other valuable things that people have placed there for safekeeping.

There are many different kinds of banks in the United States today. Some are huge institutions that control many millions of dollars and have many branch offices so their customers do not have to drive or take public transportation all the way to the main bank building to conduct their business. Others are small banks that have only one office. They don't have as many people or companies depositing their money in them, so they don't control millions of dollars. Instead, they may handle one million, or perhaps several hundred thousand, dollars. That is still quite a bit of money and responsibility!

You may wonder how a bank gets started in the first place. Banks must have money before they can open their doors for business. Where do they get the money? Is the president of the bank a rich man? Why are some people afraid to put their money in a bank? These questions, and many others, will be answered in this book.

2

BEGINNING A
BANK TODAY

*B*ANKS ARE BUSINESSES. Like any other business, they want to make money. The local grocery store makes its money selling food, and the shoe shop makes its money repairing shoes. A bank has nothing to sell and nothing to fix, so it makes its money by helping other people and companies handle *their* money.

Every business makes money at some times and loses money at other times. The money that a business makes is called its *profits*. And, logically enough, the money it loses is called its *losses*. In order for a business to succeed, it must have a lot more profits than losses. Banks, too, must make more money than they lose, or they will have to close their doors.

Suppose, when you are grown up, you decide you would like to go into the banking business. Perhaps you will decide to start a bank of your own. The first thing you will need, of course, is money, but you probably won't need as much of it as you think. $200,000 is about enough money to start a bank in a large city, and in a small town you might be able to open for business with as little as $50,000. Are you thinking, "Even $50,000 is a lot of money!"? Well, it is. But do you know it costs more than that to open a McDonald's or a Kentucky Fried Chicken restaurant?

Of course, if you are just getting started in business, you probably won't have $50,000—much less $200,000—to invest in (or put money into) your new bank. So, in order to raise the money, you have to sell shares of stock in the bank.

When people buy shares of stock in a bank—or in any business, for that matter—they are actually buying part of the business. Oh, they are not buying some of the bricks, or the front door, or the secretary's desk. That's not what we mean by owning part of a business. What they are buying is a piece of paper called a *stock certificate*. The stock certificate shows how much of a particular company you own. When you own stock in a company, you own part of that company's profits and losses. If the business succeeds and makes money, you make money, too. If the business fails and loses money, then you lose money, too. The more money you have invested, the more you can make—or lose. So, if you need $50,000 to start your bank and Carol Smith invests $25,000 in stock in the bank, she owns half the bank—and half of the profits

or losses. If Tom Drew invests \$1,000 in your bank, he owns one-fiftieth of the bank, and has a one-fiftieth share of the profits and losses.

Usually the first people to invest in a bank are the people who will become members of the Board of Directors. The people who serve on the Board of Directors of a bank are very important to the success or failure of that bank. It is they who decide how the bank conducts all of its business. All banks with the word "National" in their name (or N.A.)—for example, The First National Bank—are governed by federal law. Federal law says that all national banks must have at least five people on the Board of Directors; they may have as many as twenty-five, but no more. Members of the Board of Directors must put at least $1,000 of their own money into the bank, so they are also stockholders.

All other banks—the ones with "State" in their name, like Pasadena State Bank, and the ones with neither "National" nor "State," like Melrose Bank—are governed by the laws of the state where they are located. These laws vary from state to state, but all banks—national and state—have Boards of Directors.

Under the law, directors of a national bank can be held responsible to the stockholders if their bank loses so much money it has to go out of business. The members of the Board of Directors are responsible for the way the bank conducts all its business, and if the business is done in a sloppy, careless way and the bank has to close, it is possible for the stockholders, who have lost their investment, to sue the Board of Directors to get their money back. If the bank has no money, the members of the Board may have to pay these people out of their own pocket. So you can see how important it is that the people serving on the Board of Directors of a bank be very wise about running a business.

Members of the Board of Directors run their own businesses and do not necessarily work at the bank. Sometimes they are lawyers or merchants. Sometimes they are doctors or insurance executives. Sometimes members of the Board are retired and do not work at all.

"OUR BOARD OF DIRECTORS"

The members of the Board of Directors make the big decisions about how the bank conducts its business. But the daily running of the bank is left up to its employees.

The Board of Directors elects the *president* of the bank. Of course, he does not run for office the way the President of the United States does! He really is more or less chosen for the job. The Board selects a person to be president for many reasons. They want to choose someone whom they think will represent the bank well in the community.

The president of a bank is the person whom the newspapers, as well as the radio and television stations, talk to when they want to tell an important story about the bank. The president of the bank must be able to explain the bank's operations in words that most people can understand.

Because a bank is an important part of the community and makes its money from the people in the community, most bank presidents want to help other community organizations. Often they will serve on the Board of Directors of the Big Brothers or the Camp Fire Girls. Some bank presidents volunteer their time to help the Salvation Army or Goodwill Industries. Still, the president of a bank has other responsibilities beside talking to reporters, working with young people, or giving time to charitable organizations.

The president of a bank is directly responsible to the Board of Directors for the overall operation of the bank. He must understand how every department in the bank operates. He must understand very complicated banking laws. He attempts to get new business for the bank, too.

He visits with other business people in the community and encourages them to put their money in his bank, because that is the way his bank will grow. Of course, the bank is not really his, and neither is all the money in it. The bank belongs to the stockholders, and the money in it belongs to the people who put it there, called depositors.

Often the president of the bank is also called the "chief executive officer." That title means he is in charge of all the other officers of the bank. (By the way, even though we have been calling the bank president "he," "he" could just as easily be "she." Many women in the United States are presidents and officers of banks.)

A *bank officer* is not like a police officer or an army officer. A bank officer is elected by the Board of Directors, just as the president is. One of the jobs the bank president has is recommending that certain bank employees be elected officers. All officers of the bank, from the president on down, are employees of the bank, but not all employees of the bank are officers of it. There are many differences between an employee who is an officer and one who is not.

There are laws that govern bank officers. Bank officers must report any money they owe *anybody* to the Board of Directors. For example, if Ellen Ferguson, an officer, buys a new car with money borrowed from another bank, she must tell the bank she works for about the loan. Most people consider the amount of money they owe to be a private matter—they usually don't go around telling other people about it. But bank officers do not have that privacy. They do not have to tell their friends, but they do have to tell the Board of Directors. The Board

"I SAY, ED, OLD FELLOW, COULDN'T YOU SEE
YOUR WAY TO MAKING AN ITTY-BITTY LOAN FOR
THAT NEW DRUGSTORE ON THE CORNER?"

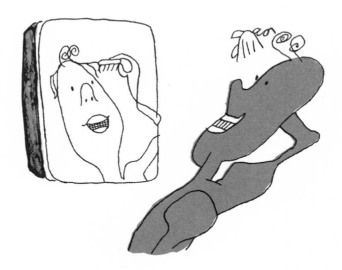

"WELL, ED, I GUESS I COULD."
"THANKS, ED."

of Directors wants to be sure that no officer of the bank owes so much money that he or she might be tempted to take some of the bank's money to pay off personal debts.

Bank officers must also tell the Board of Directors if they decide to open another business on the side. Let's say Ed Adams, the bank's loan officer, wants to buy the corner drugstore. He has someone to run the drugstore for him, and he plans to continue to work for the bank. Ed must report his purchase of the drug store to the Board of Directors. The Board of Directors must know of all business interests Ed has, because it is their responsibility to see that there is no *conflict of interest*.

A conflict of interest can occur if Ed's drugstore needs to borrow money and every other bank in town refuses to lend it. Let's say the other banks feel the drugstore is not making enough money to be able to afford to pay the loan back. Here comes the conflict of interest. Ed, a loan officer, might be tempted to loan money from *his* bank (even though he knows it isn't good banking business to do it) to his own drugstore. In a situation like this, the Board of Directors would say that the loan officer has a conflict of interest between the drugstore and the bank. The Board of Directors might ask the loan officer to choose between working for the bank and running his drugstore. They might not allow him to do both.

Employees of the bank who are not officers do not have to tell the Board of Directors about money that they borrow or outside businesses that they own. These employees do not have to report this information because they do not have the same responsibility for handling the bank's money that an officer does. The bank's officers supervise the work of all the other bank employees.

Banks employ many people for many different jobs. Banks need secretaries and bookkeepers as much as they need presidents and vice-presidents. They need employees to help keep the bank clean and employees to open the safe-deposit boxes. They need people to guard the money and people to mow the lawn.

The employee you probably see when you make a visit to the bank is the *teller*. The teller is the person who accepts your money when you want to put it into the bank. The teller also gives you money when you want to take it out. Many bankers began their banking career as tellers.

3

ALL ABOUT BANK ACCOUNTS

*E*VERY TIME YOU PUT money in the bank, you are making a *deposit*. Every time you take money out, you are making a *withdrawal*. Your money is deposited into and withdrawn from your account at the bank.

Banks offer different kinds of accounts to their customers. We will talk about checking accounts, savings accounts, and trust accounts.

Most adults, when they are paid their salaries, keep only a part of that money in their pockets or purses. They use it for bus fare, or a lunch out, or to buy a newspaper—things like that. This kind of money is called pocket change, or spending money, and most people don't keep too much of it on them. They are afraid of losing it or having it stolen.

On payday, your parents probably deposit most of their money in their accounts at the bank, where they know it will be safe. Many adults put a little money in their savings account and deposit the rest in their checking account.

You have probably seen your mom or dad writing checks to pay the household bills. A checking account is a great convenience for them. Their money is kept safely in the bank, yet they can write a check to spend some of it any time they wish.

Bankers call the money deposited in a checking account a *demand deposit*. The bank must have that money on hand at all times. When a person writes a check, he is, in a sense, demanding that his money be paid to someone (often himself).

But how many times have you said, "Mom, I need some money," and she said, "I don't *have* any," so you said, "Go cash a check," and she said, "I can't."

"MOM, GO CASH A CHECK!"

That's pretty confusing. Just yesterday the two of you were in the grocery store. As usual, you watched her pay for the groceries with a check. If she could write a check yesterday, why can't she write one today? To understand why she can't, you have to understand a little about how a checking account works.

Although it doesn't look a bit like money, a check is practically the same thing. It is a kind of fill-in-the-blank situation. Every check has a blank for the date, the *payee,* which is the person, or store, or company that is getting the money, and *two* blanks to fill in the amount of money —once in numbers and once in longhand. The bank wants to be certain it transfers the correct amount. Some people are pretty careless with their penmanship. $5.00 can look like $500 if the decimal point is missing, but written in longhand, five dollars cannot possibly

be mistaken for five hundred dollars. That's why banks want their customers to write the amount of the check both ways.

The next blank is for the signature of the person who is writing the check. Some checks have another blank that says MEMO. Sometimes people put what the check is for on this line, such as "dentist for Jay," or "new shoes for Susan."

In addition to the blanks, checks have other information printed on them. Each checking account in each bank has its own account number. That account number is printed on the check, usually somewhere at the bottom in funny-looking print that a computer reads. Besides the account number, each check in a person's checkbook usually has its own number printed in the upper right-hand corner.

No. 345

1-2345
6789

$ 5 00/XX

Dollars

J. M. Baroque

345 ⑈⑈0000006789⑈⑈

Sometimes there is a number on a check that looks a little like a fraction—you know, numbers above a line, then some numbers below. These are the bank's routing numbers. Routing numbers tell which clearing house the bank uses. We'll talk about clearing houses later.

The bank's name and address are always on the check, and most people have their name and address and telephone number printed on the checks, too.

Whoever is accepting the check—a grocery store clerk, for instance—will ask for identification, usually a driver's license or a credit card. A driver's license has an address on it, and the clerk will compare this address with the name and address printed on the check to be sure they are the same. The clerk will also look at the signature that appears on

the credit card or the driver's license. He or she will compare it to the signature on the check to be sure the check has not been forged.

Checks can be forged in two ways. Dishonest people sometimes steal checkbooks full of blank checks. Then they run around town trying to cash the checks by forging the signature of the person who owns the checkbook. Sometimes they steal checks that are already made out. In order to cash a check, the payee must *endorse* it. The payee endorses the check by signing his or her name on the back. Check thieves pretend they are the payee and forge the payee's signature on the back. Forgery is a very serious crime.

The clerk asks for identification, then, to be certain the rightful owner of the check is the person trying to pay for groceries with it. In some stores the clerks are responsible for the loss if they accept a check that has been forged or altered in any way and the bank refuses to honor it. You cannot blame them for wanting to be sure you are who you say you are!

Checks should always be written in pen, not pencil. You don't want anyone changing a check after you have written it. If someone tampers with the ink on your check, the paper changes color. When the check changes color, it is automatically voided.

Checks are much safer to carry with you than money. If you lose a ten-dollar bill, you are probably out of luck. Whoever finds it can keep it and spend it on himself. If, on the other hand, your aunt sends you a ten-dollar check for your birthday and you lose it, there is something you can do about it.

The first—and probably the hardest—thing you do is tell your aunt

PARDON MY DUST

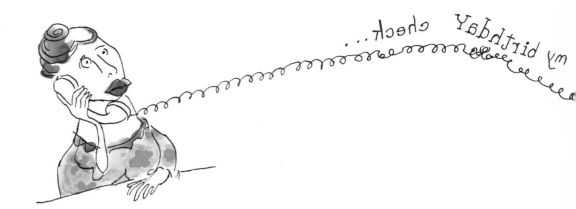

...my birthday check...

you lost the check. She then *cancels payment* on that check. When the person who writes a check cancels payment on it, the check cannot be cashed or turned in for money.

In order to cancel payment on your birthday check, your aunt notifies her bank that the check is missing. She tells the bank the check's number, how much it is for, who it is made out to, and the date that she wrote it.

The bank makes a note on your aunt's account that she wishes to cancel the payment of this check. Because it is extra work for the bank's bookkeepers to keep track of the checks its customers want canceled, the bank usually charges a small fee for this service. Once the check is canceled, even the cleverest forger will be unable to cash it, and your aunt can go ahead and write you another check to replace it. Happy Birthday at last!

You know it is illegal to forge checks, but do you know you can be penalized for writing a check for more than the balance in your checking account? If you have $100 in your checking account and you want to buy a new bike for $110, it is illegal to write a check for $110—

even if you plan to hurry on down to the bank with the extra $10.00! When someone writes a check for more money than he has in his account, he is *overdrawing* his checking account. The bank penalizes customers who overdraw their checking accounts by charging them a fee of several dollars.

It is illegal to deliberately overdraw your checking account. But sometimes people overdraw their checking accounts accidently. They make careless mistakes as they add and subtract in their *check register*. The check register is given to you, along with blank checks, when you open a checking account. The check register has places to record all the information about the checks you write. You can record the check number, the date you write it, who you write it to, and how much money you write it for. The check register has columns that help you keep track of exactly how much money you have in your checking account. The "balance forward" column shows how much money is in your account to start with. The "deposit" column shows any money you add to your account. All the checks that you write are subtracted from your balance.

Think for a minute about the ten-dollar birthday check from your aunt. If your aunt had $100 in her checking account before she wrote you that check, she would show $100.00 in the "balance forward" column in her check register. Then she would record the ten-dollar check to you. Now she has $10.00 less in her account, so she would subtract $10.00 from $100, leaving her with a new balance of $90.00.

As your aunt writes other checks for other things, she keeps subtracting them from her balance. When the balance gets so low that she cannot write another check, she must make a deposit to add more money to her account. When your mother says she can't cash a check, it probably means that she has used up all the money in her "balance" column, and she must deposit more money in the bank before she can cash any more checks.

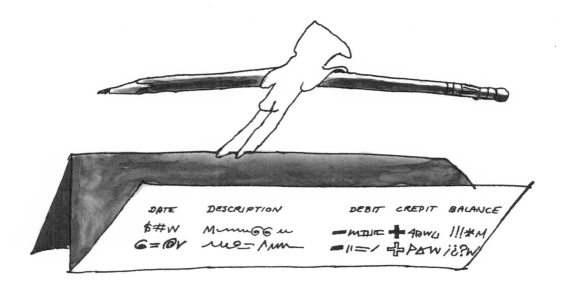

Each month the bank sends each checking-account customer something called a balance sheet or statement. The balance sheet shows exactly what checks have been subtracted from the account and what money has been added during the month. The figures on the balance sheet the bank sends should match the figures that have been recorded in the check register. Most people *balance* their checkbook every month. When your parents compare the figures in the check register with the figures on the balance sheet from the bank, they are balancing their checkbook.

Checking accounts are not the only accounts banks offer. People also deposit their money in savings accounts. There are short-term savings accounts and long-term savings accounts. Short-term savings accounts are called *passbook savings accounts*, and long-term savings accounts are usually called *certificates of deposit.*

Many boys and girls have passbook savings accounts. They deposit their birthday money in them, money they earn from any jobs they may have, and maybe part of their allowance. When someone opens a passbook savings account, he or she is issued a passbook. A passbook looks a little like a check register, but it doesn't have exactly the same information in it.

Most passbooks will have columns for the date, the amount of deposits, and the amount of withdrawals. There is also a place for the current balance in the account. Some banks offer passbooks made so that you fill in this information yourself—just as you do in a checkbook. Other banks offer passbooks that the teller places in a special machine, which prints the information about your deposit or withdrawal and your new balance right on the page of your passbook.

A passbook savings account is easy to deposit money into and easy to withdraw money from. You can open a passbook savings account with as little as $5.00. You can withdraw your money from it just about any time you want. It is a short-term savings account.

Remember that bankers call the money people deposit in their checking accounts demand deposits. The money people deposit in their savings accounts is called *time deposits*. Banks pay *interest*, or extra money, on time deposits. (Some demand deposits earn interest too.)

You may have to give the bank a little warning if you want to withdraw the money from your savings account. If your money is in a short-term savings account, you may not have to give any warning at all. But if you have your money in a long-term savings account, such as a certificate of deposit, you may have to notify the bank a few days before you intend to withdraw it. Why? Because the bank has put that money out to work for you, and it may need a little time to get it back.

When you put your money in a certificate of deposit, you promise to leave it in the bank for a certain period of time. You do not make that kind of agreement when you put your money in a passbook savings account. There are other differences between short-term passbook accounts and long-term certificates of deposit.

Normally, there is a minimum amount of money that you can put into a certificate of deposit. You usually cannot put less than $50.00 into one. Many are for $5,000 or $10,000! Certificates of deposit earn more interest than passbook savings do because the people have prom-

ised not to withdraw the money for a while. Depending on the amount of the certificate, you promise to leave your money for as little as thirty days or as long as several years. Generally, the longer you agree to leave your money, the more interest the bank will pay you. If you have an emergency and you *must* withdraw your certificates of deposit before the agreed-upon time is up, the bank will penalize you by lowering the amount of interest it will pay on them.

We have talked about checking accounts and savings accounts. There is a third kind of account that banks offer their customers to help them handle their money. It is called a trust account, and the name is a good one. The name came about because people *entrusted* their money or their property to the bank. They wanted the bank to handle it for them. Some banks have "Trust" in their name, like the First National Bank and Trust Company.

A bank's trust department offers many services. It can invest money in stocks and bonds for you. If your parents own an apartment house, it can collect the rent for them. Sometimes it advises people how to draw up a will.

Many parents set up a trust account for their young children in their will. Then, if the parents die while the children are still too young to handle money, the bank does it for them. The bank becomes the *trustee* of the children's money until they are old enough to take over for themselves.

Banks do not offer trust services for free. They charge a fee to handle people's money, and it is usually a percentage of the money they handle.

4

BUDDY, CAN YOU SPARE A DIME?

or

I'll Pay You Back Tomorrow

ONCE THERE WAS A LITTLE girl who had ten silver dollars. She took them to her bank and deposited them in her savings account. A few months later the girl wanted to buy something with her own money, so she went to the bank to withdraw $5.00 from her savings account. The teller at the bank checked the balance in her account, saw that she had more than five dollars in her account, smiled and handed the girl a five-dollar bill.

"I want my silver dollars!" she yelled. "You give me my silver dollars! I don't want this yukky paper money! I want *my* money! What did you do with my money?" She thought her silver dollars were just waiting there in the vault—waiting for her to come and get them when she decided to spend them.

37

Her money was waiting for her, of course. She did get $5.00 out of her savings account, but it wasn't the same $5.00 she put in.

Banks have records that show how much money people have in their accounts, but they don't keep money separate in special little jars

labeled with each customer's name. Instead, the ten silver dollars the girl deposited in her savings account were put in a big sack with all the other money the bank collected that day. Her balance sheet showed that she had deposited $10.00 in her account, but when she wanted to withdraw $5.00 a few months later, her silver dollars were no longer there. They had been put out to work. One way that a bank makes money work is by lending it to someone else.

Stockholders · individuals · businesses

College $?

Money for bank loans

Before you can lend money, however, you have to have some—right? A bank gets the money that it lends from different places. The bank uses the money that the stockholders have invested to make loans. It also lends the money that individuals and businesses have deposited in their savings accounts.

Banks loan money to different people for different reasons. They loan money to individuals to buy things like homes and cars and boats. They loan money to people to start a business, or to help an already established business grow.

Before a banker decides to loan someone money to buy a home or a car or a boat, he makes sure those items are worth what they cost. No bank would lend someone $1,000 to buy a car that is only worth $800. What if the person couldn't pay the loan back? The bank could *repossess* the car—that is, take it away from the person who had it—but if it can be sold for only $800 the bank would lose $200. That's no way to run a business!

When a bank loans people money to buy *things*, such as houses or cars or boats, the bank keeps the *title* to those things until the loans are paid back. A title is a legal document that says who really owns something. When a bank lends someone money to buy property, such as a house, the bank holds a *mortgage* on the property. A mortgage is a claim on the property until the loan is paid back.

YOU HAVEN'T MADE ONE SINGLE PAYMENT TOWARD THE LOAN FOR THAT SUB. GIVE IT BACK!

What if someone wants to borrow money to put a fence around his back yard? The bank would not hold title to the fence—what good would that do? The bank can't sell the fence if the loan isn't paid. A fence needs a yard to go with it. When people borrow money to buy something the bank cannot easily repossess, like a fence or a new busi-

ness, the bank usually asks them to put up *collateral*. Collateral is a kind of pledge that the money will be repaid. For example, if Mr. Jones wants to borrow $1,000 to fence in his back yard, he can put up his thousand-dollar riding lawn mower as collateral. Mr. Jones can still ride his lawn mower around his newly fenced yard, but he cannot sell his lawn mower or give it away until the loan for the fence is paid back. If Mr. Jones fails to pay his loan back, the bank can take his lawnmower and sell it.

Banks don't want to repossess anything they have loaned people money to buy. Banks don't want houses or used cars, boats or lawn-mowers. So before a bank loans anyone money, it looks at the person—or company—very carefully. A bank wants to know how the person or company plans to pay the money back. Does the person have a job? Does the person or company have an account with the bank? Is the company making money? These are some of the questions the loan officer at the bank will ask.

Having a job or making a profit in business may not guarantee getting a loan. The bank will want to be certain that the person or company is making *enough* money to pay the loan back. After all, if your allowance is 50¢ a week, you cannot pay 75¢ a week on a loan payment, can you?

A person's or business's *credit rating* is another important thing a banker will look at before he decides to loan money. Any time you borrow money or pay for something over a period of time instead of right away, you are buying on credit. The only way to establish a credit rating is by buying something on credit. Your credit rating shows whether you can be counted on to pay what is owed.

A good credit rating is a very valuable thing to have. A poor credit rating may show that you often skip a payment, or make it late, or, possibly, refuse to pay at all! A poor credit rating may keep you from being able to borrow money when you need it.

The members of the Board of Directors of each bank decide how the bank will loan money and who will be allowed to borrow it. These rules about loans are called the bank's loan policy. The Board of Directors works hard to be certain that the bank's loans will be good ones that are paid back completely and on time.

"IT'S OK, MOM, I'M
ESTABLISHING A CREDIT RATING."

5

HOW YOUR MONEY
EARNS MONEY

ONCE THE LOAN OFFICER
at the bank decides to lend someone money, legal papers called a loan contract have to be filled out. The loan contract states who is borrowing the money, how much is being borrowed, how long it will take to pay it back, and what the monthly payments will be. If the loan is guaranteed (or *secured*) by collateral, that information is included in the contract, too. The loan officer at the bank and the person who is borrowing the money sign the loan contract. Then the bank gives the borrower his money.

Each month the borrower pays the bank some of the money until finally the loan is paid off. If you borrowed $100 for only one month, you might find that, at the end of the month, you had to pay the bank $101. "Why, that's more than I borrowed," you may say. You are

*Sam's Bank pays interest on its customers' savings
accounts and receives interest on the money it loans.*

right. That extra $1.00 you are paying is interest on the loan, a fee for the privilege of using someone else's money.

Remember when we said that the bank pays interest on your time deposits—your savings accounts? The bank pays you for the privilege of using your money to lend to someone else.

The interest that banks pay on savings accounts varies with the kind of account it is. If it is a simple passbook savings account that does not require you to leave your money for a specific length of time, the bank will probably pay you around 5 percent interest. Therefore, if you leave $100 in a passbook account for one year, at the end of that time you will have $105.50 in your account.

If you put your liquid assets—that is, your money—in a certificate of deposit the bank will pay a higher interest rate. Instead of 5½ percent, your money can earn interest of over 6 or 7 percent, depending on how long you leave your money in the bank.

The bank pays you interest on your savings, and it charges you interest when you make a loan. It works like this. Suppose Beth, your little sister, has $10.00 saved up, and she isn't planning to spend it right away. You say, "I'd like to use your $10.00 this month. I'll pay you 6 percent interest each month, and at the end of one month you'll have $10.60, instead of just $10.00." She thinks it over and agrees to the deal. Then Alex, your friend across the street, says he wants to borrow $10.00 from you to buy a part for his bike. You tell him, "I'll lend you the $10.00, but I'm going to charge you 10 percent interest each month

for the loan. At the end of the month you'll have to pay me $11.00."
Alex really wants that bike part, so he agrees to the terms of your loan.

At the end of the month Alex brings you eleven one-dollar bills in payment of his loan. He has established a good credit rating with you! You take the money and pay Beth $10.60, as you promised to do. Now you have established a good credit rating, too, *and* 40¢ profit left to put in your pocket—thanks to interest. Your sister's $10.00 has been out working. Because you paid her 6 percent interest for the privilege of using her money, it earned her an extra 60¢, and because you charged your friend more interest than you paid your sister, it earned you 40¢.

Although this is a very simple explanation, banks make money in much the same way. They charge their customers more interest to borrow money than they pay on their savings.

There are other ways that banks put money to work. They can invest in *bonds*, just as individuals and other businesses do, and, in a few special cases, in stocks.

We know that banks, and other companies, too, are financed by people who are willing to buy shares of stock in them. But individuals are not the only ones who buy stock in banks and other businesses. Sometimes banks buy stock in other companies, and other companies buy stock in banks. These businesses are investing their profits in other businesses. The money they invest helps the business grow. When a company is successful, the value of its stock usually increases. Sometimes the company pays its stockholders a *dividend* on the shares of stock

Sam's Bank invests some money in stock in a wishing well company. As a stockholder, the bank receives a dividend from the company's profits.

The bank pays dividends from its own profits to the people and the companies who are its stockholders.

they own. A dividend is extra money, different from interest in that it represents part of the company's profit.

However, companies are not the only corporations that need money to help them grow. It may surprise you to know that cities and towns also need money to grow on. But a city can't sell stock when it needs money for new streets or fire engines. A city just can't sell a part of itself! However it can sell bonds.

A city sells bonds to *investors*—people or companies who are interested in seeing their money earn money. When an investor buys a thousand-dollar bond, the city can use the $1,000 for a specific period of time, usually several years. The city, in turn, promises to pay interest on the bond until the bond *matures*. The bond matures at the end of

the time specified. Then the investor can cash it and get his money back. Of course, he will also have the interest that bond money has earned over the years.

Now you can see that stocks are certificates that show that you *own* something, and bonds are certificates that show that somebody *owes* you something. People and companies invest money in stocks and bonds because they realize that the money they invest can earn even more money for them, thanks to dividends and interest. Of course, there is always the chance that you can lose money by investing in stocks and bonds. If a company fails, its stock will be worth nothing, and if a city *forfeits* its bonds—if it cannot pay the investors their money when the bonds mature—the investors will lose their money, also. A wise investor studies carefully before putting money into anything. Both stocks and bonds can make—or lose—you money!

6

IF A BANK RAN OUT
OF MONEY . . .

*B*Y NOW YOU MAY ASK, "What if the bank loaned out all its money (including what *I've* got in *my* savings account) and lots of people didn't pay their loans back? The bank wouldn't be able to give me my money when I asked for it. That would be awful!"

Don't worry. By law, no bank is allowed to lend all of its money to people. Banks must keep a certain amount of their deposits on *reserve*. Reserves are the bank's liquid assets—money that they can get their hands on right away. So if you want to withdraw all the money in your savings account tomorrow, the bank should be able to give it to you.

It wasn't always this way, however. At one time banks did not keep enough money on reserve, and they got into trouble. It happened like this: Right after World War I the prices of goods and services in the

United States began to rise. When the price of things seems to be going up, up, up, people say we are having *inflation*. During a period of inflation, many people rush to buy today the things they will soon want because they are afraid that if they wait, the items will cost even *more* tomorrow.

All through the 1920s, stocks continued to rise in price. People hurried to buy stock in different companies. They thought they had better buy the stock at $10.00 a share because by the next week the price might rise to $15.00 a share. If they owned a hundred shares of the stock, they could make a quick profit of $500 in one week. There is nothing wrong with making money like this. Individuals and businesses do it all the time.

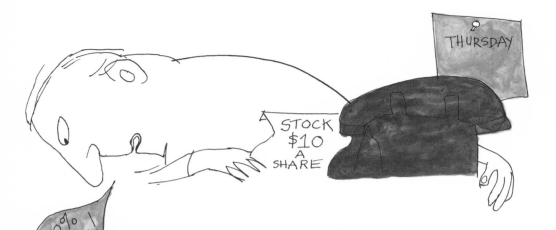

But back in the 1920s, there were no federal laws to cover investing in the stock market. People who really didn't have the $10.00 it took to buy a share of stock were allowed to buy it anyway. *Stockbrokers*—the people who sell stock—allowed people to buy stock on *margin*. In the 1920s, the margin was often only 10 percent. In other words, if you wanted to buy that ten dollar stock and you didn't have $10.00 just then, the stockbroker might allow you to give him 10 percent of the stock's value as a down payment and you could owe him the rest. (By the way, the stockbroker would charge interest on the amount you still owed him.) You would be buying the stock on a 90 percent margin. In this case, you would send $1.00 to your broker, and he would send you your share of stock. Then the next week, when the price went up to $15.00, you could call him on the phone and tell him to sell your stock. When he did, he would deduct the $9.00 margin that you still owed, the interest that he charged on that money, and his small fee for selling the stock. When all these charges were subtracted from $15.00,

you would still have a nice profit, probably around $5.00, and you would have spent only a dollar of your own money to get it.

During the time we are talking about, lots of people and companies and banks invested their money in the stock market in just this way. They did not keep any money on reserve for an emergency. Suddenly—and no one knows exactly why—people quit buying stocks and began to sell them to get their profit. The price of the stocks, instead of continuing to go up, began to drop. Stockbrokers quickly asked investors to pay their margin account—that is, to pay the money they still owed. If you didn't *have* the $9.00 you owed on your share of stock, the stockbroker could take your share of stock and sell it. Of course, because of the falling prices, your stock was not worth $10.00 any more—but you still owed $9.00 on it. Your stock might not have been worth even $5.00. The value of some stocks fell to practically nothing. Obviously people who had invested in the market were losing money. And so were banks.

In 1929 the stock market crashed in the United States. Many people lost all the money they had invested in shares of stock in companies. Without shareholders' money, many of these companies could not operate, so people lost their jobs. Without a job, no one could earn any

money to invest in companies. It was a terrible time for people in the United States. People refer to this time as the Great Depression.

During the Great Depression, everyone who had money in a bank wanted to withdraw it. They needed it to buy food and clothing. They all wanted their money *immediately*. Remember, we have said that a bank doesn't keep all its customers' money right there in its vaults; some is put to work earning interest on loans and investments. Many banks had taken too much of their reserve to invest in the stock market, and it was gone, so the banks could not give every depositor his money that very day. The banks simply did not have the money in their vaults.

Angry crowds of depositors formed outside the doors of many banks. They demanded their money. When practically all the depositors in a particular bank demand their money at one time, the situation is called a *run* on the bank. A run can cause a bank to *fail*—that is, run out of money and close its doors.

During the Great Depression, there were thousands of runs on thousands of banks. From 1929 until 1933 over five thousand banks in this country failed and had to close their doors. The people who had money in those banks lost it.

Franklin D. Roosevelt was inaugurated President of the United States on March 4, 1933. He realized that something had to be done to stop the runs on the country's banks. Practically every bank in the country was in danger of failing. People no longer trusted their banks, so they all wanted to withdraw their gold and silver and their paper money, too.

"TERRIBLY SORRY, EVERYONE—BANK'S CLOSED."

The banks that were still in business had to have a chance to get hold of some of the money that they had invested. So, less than forty-eight hours after he became President, Franklin Roosevelt closed all this country's banks for four days.

President Roosevelt did not tell anyone ahead of time that he was going to close the banks. Many people did not have much money in their pockets when the closing happened. Without the banks, people could not cash a check or withdraw money from their savings accounts.

But nobody panicked when the banks closed. People used different things for money. In Salt Lake City, one man traded a pair of slacks for a ticket on a trolley. Slacks became his medium of exchange. In Oklahoma City, a hotel agreed to let its guests settle their bills during this time by trading for anything the hotel could use in its coffee shop. One person brought in a pig! So a pig became a medium of exchange instead of a few dollars.

When the banks closed for four days, the people in this country calmed down a little. The new President told Americans he had a plan to help this country's banks.

His plan was called the Emergency Banking Act, and Congress quickly passed it on March 9, 1933. As soon as the Emergency Banking Act was passed, the banks that had good management and were run by good businessmen began to open their doors once again.

7

KEEPING YOUR MONEY
SAFE AND SOUND

*T*HERE ARE PEOPLE ALIVE today who remember when President Roosevelt had to close all the banks. Some of these people lost all their money. Some are still afraid to put their money in a bank. Every once in a while you hear about someone who has stuffed his money in a mattress or buried it in a can in the back yard. That's too bad. Mattresses can catch on fire and tin cans can rust. Besides, money tucked away in mattresses and cans doesn't go to work earning interest.

Today, most bank accounts are insured, or protected, by the Federal Deposit Insurance Corporation, or F.D.I.C., so very few people have to worry about losing their money if their bank fails. The next time you go to your bank, look for a sign that says MEMBER, F.D.I.C. I bet you'll find it. Most banks in our country are members of the F.D.I.C.

The Federal Deposit Insurance Corporation is part of the Banking Act of 1933. President Roosevelt signed the Banking Act of 1933 on June 16th of that year. The law that he had signed earlier, in March, 1933, right after he was inaugurated, was called the *Emergency* Banking Act of 1933. It was a good name for the law, because there really was an emergency at the time. However, by June, the people of America had calmed down and Congress had had time to think of more banking laws to help this country's banks be safer and stronger. They put all these laws, including the establishment of the F.D.I.C., into the Banking Act of 1933. Banks that are members of the F.D.I.C. guarantee that their customers' money is safe—up to a certain limit. The money is safe because it is insured by the Federal Government. Banks who are members of F.D.I.C. insure their customers' deposits up to $100,000. If your bank failed and you had $100,000 or less in your account, the Federal Deposit Insurance Corporation would see to it that you got your money back.

All national banks must be members of the F.D.I.C. State banks may choose to become a member or not. Most banks want this kind of protection for their customers' money, so practically all the banks in this country join the F.D.I.C.

Besides being a member of the F.D.I.C., all national banks must belong to the Federal Reserve System, too. The Federal Reserve System operates banks that are different from the kind of banks we have talked about up till now. We have been talking about the kind of bank that is located in your neighborhood. It is called a commercial bank, and it exists to make money and to serve the needs of people like you and your family.

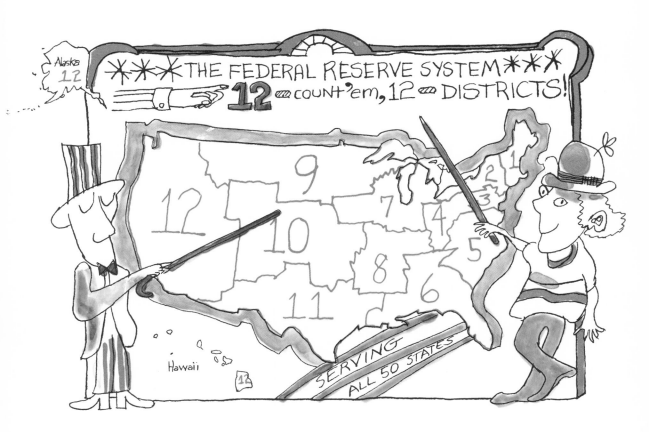

There is another kind of bank in this country, too. It is called the central bank, and it serves the needs of the commercial banks. It is a government service and is not in business to make money for itself. The United States Federal Reserve System is this country's central bank. It was established in 1913 and has twelve Federal Reserve banks, one in each of the twelve Federal Reserve districts of the United States: Boston, New York, Philadelphia, Richmond, Atlanta, Cleveland, Chicago, St. Louis, Kansas City, Minneapolis, Dallas, and San Francisco.

The Federal Reserve System runs the Federal Reserve banks. All national banks must belong to the Federal Reserve System. State banks can choose whether they want to belong to it or not.

The Federal Reserve System is very important to this country's economy. It is headed by a Board of Governors—*not* a Board of Directors. The President of the United States appoints the members of the Board of Governors, and he also appoints the person who will serve as Chairman of the Board. All members of the Board of Governors have their offices in Washington, D.C.   cop. 2

The Federal Reserve Board has the power to tell the commercial banks the maximum amount of interest they can pay to depositors.

Sometimes even a commercial bank needs to borrow money to keep its business going. The Federal Reserve banks lend money to commercial banks.

The Federal Reserve banks also help commercial banks by acting as clearing houses for all the thousands of checks that must be processed each day. Remember when we talked about the routing number—the one that looks like a funny fraction—on a check? The routing number tells which of the twelve Federal Reserve banks that check should be sent to for credit.

We have already seen how complicated checking accounts can be. Your family may have only one checking account to keep up with. Your commercial bank has thousands. The Federal Reserve bank helps your bank handle many of its checks.

Do you ever wonder what happened to the second birthday check your aunt sent you—the one you didn't lose? Well, after you cashed it, the bank looked at the routing number on that check and sent it off

to the correct Federal Reserve bank. The Federal Reserve bank took your aunt's check and sent your bank the $10.00. In a way, you could say it cashed the check for your bank. So now your bank has been reimbursed for the $10.00 that it gave you. Next, the Federal Reserve bank sent the check to your aunt's bank. Your aunt's bank deducted $10.00 from her checking account (she had already done this in her check register) and sent the $10.00 on to the Federal Reserve bank. Then your aunt's bank punched the check with tiny little holes that read PAID if you hold it up to the light. The check is canceled and cannot be used again.

Suppose a check cannot be paid. Suppose there is not enough money in the account to pay it. What happens to the check then?

Your aunt's check is sent to the Federal Reserve bank for her district.

...which sends it to your aunt's bank. PAID.

Slang for a check that cannot be paid is *rubber check*: A rubber check is said to *bounce* (also slang), and in a way it does—right back to the payee, and eventually to the person who wrote it.

Suppose you sell your bike for $50.00, and the person who buys it pays you with an out-of-town check. You take that check to your bank and deposit it in your checking account. We know now that your bank will send that check on to the Federal Reserve bank, which will, in turn, pay your bank $50.00 for it. Then the Federal Reserve bank sends it on to the bicycle-buyer's bank for *collection*—another word for payment. If there is not enough money in the bicycle-buyer's account to pay the check, the bank has two choices, and it has twenty-four hours to decide between them.

Each morning a bank officer reviews the checks that have come in the day before and are drawn on accounts that have insufficient funds to pay them. *Insufficient funds* (or ISF) is the correct banking term both for an account that does not have enough money to pay the check and for the check itself. The officer must decide whether the bank will go ahead and pay the ISF check anyway and try to collect the money from its customer, or return the check to the person who accepted it in the first place. According to the banking laws, if the officer does not return the check within twenty-four hours, the bank *must* pay it— whether it can collect the money from its customer or not. Decisions like this are part of a bank officer's job.

If the bank's customer is a responsible person who rarely overdraws his account, the officer may decide to go ahead and pay the check. Then the officer calls the customer and tells him that the bank has done him this favor. The officer asks the customer to bring money to the bank right away to cover the check. If the customer brings the money, whoever accepted his check will never know that there were insufficient funds to cover it.

The other choice, or decision, the bank officer may make is to return his customer's check to you. If the officer decides to do that, the bank returns the bicycle-buyer's check to the Federal Reserve bank, which then sends it back to your bank. Your bank takes the $50.00 it had put in your account when you deposited that check *out* of your account and returns the check to you with a note on it marked INSUFFICIENT FUNDS. Now you can see why rubber checks are said to bounce!

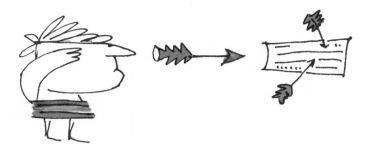

What are you going to do now? Somebody has your bike, and you have a check that isn't worth any money.

The first thing you can do—if you were careful about getting identification when you accepted the check—is get in touch with the person who wrote it. Sometimes people make mistakes, and they will be happy to write you another check (if you're willing to take it!) or to bring you the $50.00 in cash.

If you cannot reach the person, you can take the check to your bank and leave it for collection. Handling checks left for collection is another service the bank offers its customers. Your bank will notify the bicycle-buyer's bank that you are waiting to collect your money for this check. The bicycle-buyer's bank (we should say B.B.B., shouldn't we?) will check the bicycle-buyer's account each day. Checks left for collection are paid on a first-come, first-served basis, so if yours is the first one waiting to be paid, as soon as the bicycle-buyer has $50.00 in his account, your check will be cashed and you will get your money. Of course, if your check is fourth in line and the money in his account runs out before you are paid, you may be out of luck—and $50.00.

Usually your bank will hold that check in their collection department for ten or fifteen days while it tries to collect your money for you. If the check still cannot be paid at the end of that time, your bank will probably return it to you, and you, very likely, will be more cautious about accepting a check from someone the next time you sell something.

If you have a checking account, each month you will receive an envelope from the bank. The envelope contains all of your checks that the bank has paid that month, and your account's balance sheet. These checks may have traveled far before coming back to you. The Federal Reserve banks help send the checks where they need to go. Trillions of dollars worth of checks are handled by the Federal Reserve Banks each year.

This machine prepares monthly checking account statements.

There is one other very important thing that the federal government does for banks. It sees that their books are examined regularly by Federal Reserve Bank examiners. If a bank is not a member of the Federal Reserve System, its books are examined by bankers from the state banking commission of the state where the bank is located.

Bank examiners do not tell the bank's officers when they are coming to examine the books. If anyone who is working in the bank is dishonest, the examiners do not want that person to have a chance to cover up what he has been doing.

When the bank examiners arrive, the bank must let them see all its records. The bank examiners go over everything about the bank and its business procedures very carefully. It takes a long time to do this— a week for a small bank, much longer for a large one.

If the examiners think that the bank has not been careful enough about the people it is lending money to, they tell it so. When the examiners are satisfied that the bank is operating carefully, they leave. If the examiners discover that the bank is being run so poorly that it is in danger of failing, they can order it to close. Another group of businessmen would probably take over the bank, and the customers' money would remain safe.

The job of the bank examiners is to make certain that banks do all they can to protect their customers' money. Thanks to the two Banking Acts of 1933, banks are much safer today than they were when your grandparents were young.

Today, money belongs in banks that are made of bricks and concrete—not ones that are shaped like little pigs.